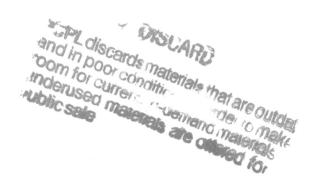

CIVIL RIGHTS LEADERS

MEET CORETTA SCOTT KING

MELODY S. MIS

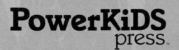

PowerKiDS press.

New York

To old friends, Jack & Barbara Shelton

Published in 2008 by The Rosen Publishing Group, Inc.
29 East 21st Street, New York, NY 10010

First Edition

Editor: Nicole Pristash and Jennifer Way
Book Design: Julio Gil
Photo Researcher: Nicole Pristash

Photo Credits: Cover, back cover, title page, headers, pp. 5, 7, 9, 11, 13, 21 © Getty Images; pp. 15, 17, 19 © Associated Press.

Library of Congress Cataloging-in-Publication Data

Mis, Melody S.
   Meet Coretta Scott King / Melody S. Mis. — 1st ed.
      p. cm. — (Civil rights leaders)
   Includes bibliographical references and index.
   ISBN 978-1-4042-4211-1 (library binding)
   1. King, Coretta Scott, 1927–2006—Juvenile literature. 2. African American women civil rights workers—Biography—Juvenile literature. 3. Civil rights workers—United States—Biography—Juvenile literature. 4. African Americans—Biography—Juvenile literature. 5. King, Martin Luther, Jr., 1929–1968—Juvenile literature. 6. African Americans—Civil rights—History—20th century—Juvenile literature. 7. Civil rights movements—United States—History—20th century—Juvenile literature. I. Title.
   E185.97.K47M57 2008
   323.092—dc22
   [B]
                                            2007034650

Manufactured in the United States of America

Contents

Meet Coretta Scott King

Coretta Scott King is often called the mother of the **civil rights movement**. She worked beside her husband, Martin Luther King Jr., as he led the struggle to get equal rights for African Americans. After his death, in 1968, Scott King started the King Center, to honor her husband's work.

Scott King spent the rest of her life working for world peace and equality. She gave speeches and led **protests**. She also spoke with world leaders about the needs of the poor. Her hard work helped change many people's beliefs.

The civil rights movement was a period of time in the 1950s and 1960s during which people protested against African-American inequality. At this time, black people did not have the same rights as white people. The civil rights movement helped change that.

Coretta Scott King taught people about love and equality. Like her husband, she helped the world become a more peaceful place.

The Segregated South

Coretta Scott was born on April 27, 1927, on a farm near Marion, Alabama. As a child, she worked in her family's garden and fed their farm animals. To make money for school, Coretta picked cotton on nearby farms.

During this time, the South practiced **segregation**. White people in the South did not believe blacks should have equal rights. They did not want blacks to go to school or be successful. When she was young, Coretta's father bought a new home for the family. It was burned down. It is believed that some white men set it on fire.

The Jim Crow laws controlled segregation. These laws stated that blacks and whites had to be kept away from each other. They could not eat in the same places or use the same bathrooms as white people. Also, if a public bus got full, blacks had to give up their seats to whites.

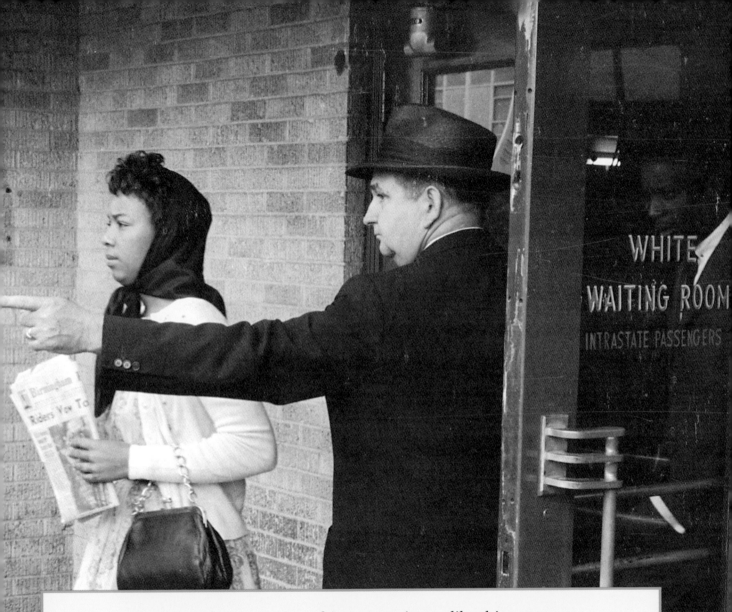

WHITE
WAITING ROOM
INTRASTATE PASSENGERS

Because of segregation, African Americans, like this woman, were not allowed to wait in the same public places as whites.

Going to School

Coretta's parents saved money to send their children to school because they believed it was important. Coretta was a good student. She went to Antioch College in Ohio. Coretta was one of the first African Americans to attend Antioch. After she finished, she studied music at the New England Conservatory of Music, in Boston, Massachusetts.

While Coretta was in Boston, she met Martin Luther King Jr. He wanted to marry her soon after they met. She was not sure she wanted to marry because she wanted to be a **concert** singer. Coretta was soon won over by him, though.

Coretta Scott King did not plan on working for the civil rights movement. When she met her husband, though, she realized how important the cause was to her. Here, the couple is shown visiting the United Nations in New York City.

Coretta Scott married Martin Luther King Jr. in 1953. They moved to Montgomery, Alabama. King led the civil rights movement there. Together, he and Scott King helped African Americans gain equal rights through **nonviolence**.

The two led many peaceful marches. Scott King also used her music to protest unfair laws by giving **freedom** concerts. Some white people, however, did not like blacks protesting for equal rights. Some of them tried to harm the Kings. Scott King was worried that her husband and their four children might be hurt or killed. Sadly, this did come true.

At freedom concerts, Coretta Scott King sang songs and read stories to tell others about the civil rights movement. These concerts were given to groups of people in American cities.

In 1965, Coretta Scott King and her husband led a protest march from Selma, Alabama, to Montgomery, Alabama. This march was an important step toward peacefully getting blacks the right to vote.

On April 4, 1968, Martin Luther King Jr. was in Memphis to lead a march. A white man shot King and killed him. This upset many people. Coretta Scott King stayed strong, though.

She decided to spend the rest of her life keeping her husband's dream of equality living. She spoke at a march only a month after King was killed. She also joined the Mother's March, to get help for poor families. As well as marches, Scott King spoke to groups all over the world about nonviolence and civil rights. She was getting the message of equality and peace to the people.

In 1968, Coretta Scott King led the Poor People's March in Washington, D.C. This protest centered on the needs of the poor of every race, not just blacks.

Coretta Scott King was proud of her husband's accomplishments. Because of his work, the U.S. government passed laws that gave African Americans the same rights that whites had. Scott King planned a **memorial** center to honor King and his work. It is called the King Center. It opened in Atlanta, Georgia, in 1981.

The King Center is the first memorial of its kind to be built for an African-American leader. The purpose of the center is to teach others about King's ideas about equality and peace. Visitors can take classes on nonviolence, read about the history of the civil rights movement, and visit King's grave.

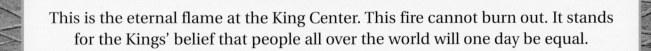

This is the eternal flame at the King Center. This fire cannot burn out. It stands for the Kings' belief that people all over the world will one day be equal.

Coretta Scott King believed that the United States should honor her husband and his work for civil rights. She wanted the government to make Martin Luther King Jr.'s birthday a national holiday. She spent 10 years asking people to help her get this done. In 1983, Congress at last passed the law that made the third Monday in January Martin Luther King Jr. Day. It was the first time in the nation's history that an African American had been honored in this way.

Americans **celebrated** the first Martin Luther King Jr. holiday in 1986. Since then, more than 100 countries have celebrated this holiday.

In 1985, Coretta Scott King announced that the first Martin Luther King Jr. Day would take place on January 20, 1986.

As Coretta Scott King grew older, she remained busy in the struggle for civil rights and world peace. In 1985, she was **arrested** in Washington, D.C., for protesting against segregation in South Africa. Scott King visited South Africa the next year. She wanted to visit the South Africans who were fighting for equal rights.

Scott King also spoke out about other topics, such as women's rights and war. Until her death, Scott King worked to make the world a better and safer place.

The protest and arrest of Coretta Scott King (front center), shown here, brought much-needed attention to South Africa's struggle against segregation.

Coretta Scott King has received many **awards** and honors for her work. She was the first woman to give a speech at St. Paul's Cathedral in London, England. She was also the first woman to speak to students at Harvard University's Class Day. Scott King received the Ceres Award from the United Nations for trying to help poor people all over the world. She was named Woman of the Year in 1960 and 1968.

Scott King's highest honor was having an award named after her. The Coretta Scott King Award is given to African Americans who **inspire** others by writing or drawing children's books.

In 2005, Coretta Scott King was given the Hero Award. It was given to her by the Recording Academy, for her work to help the poor and for equal rights.

In 2005, Coretta Scott King began to have heart problems. She died on January 14, 2006, at age 78, in a hospital in Mexico. She was buried next to her husband at the King Center.

Coretta Scott King will be remembered as one of the United States' most important civil rights leaders. She raised four children and wrote three books, all while doing whatever work was necessary to end segregation. Her fight for equality in schools, housing, and jobs helped change people's hearts and the nation's laws.

Glossary

arrested (uh-REST-ed) To have been stopped from doing a crime.

awards (uh-WORDZ) Special honors that are given to people to reward them for something.

celebrated (SEH-leh-brayt-ed) Honored something by doing special things.

civil rights (SIH-vul RYTS) The rights that citizens have.

concert (KONT-sert) A musical performance.

freedom (FREE-dum) The state of being free.

inspire (in-SPY-ur) To fill with an emotion or an idea that helps others.

memorial (meh-MOR-ee-ul) Something built to remember a person.

movement (MOOV-ment) A group of people who get together to back the same cause or purpose.

nonviolence (non-VY-uh-lents) Without using bodily force against someone or something.

protests (PROH-tests) Acts of disagreement.

segregation (seh-grih-GAY-shun) The act of keeping one group of people apart from another group of people.

Index

Web Sites

Due to the changing nature of Internet links, PowerKids Press has developed an online list of Web sites related to the subject of this book. This site is updated regularly. Please use this link to access the list: www.powerkidslinks.com/crl/csk/